Skipping in the Street

First published in 2009
by Wayland

This paperback edition published in 2010 by Wayland

Text copyright © Anna Matthew
Illustration copyright © Heather Heyworth

Wayland
338 Euston Road
London NW1 3BH

Wayland Australia
Level 17/207 Kent Street
Sydney, NSW 2000

The rights of Anna Matthew to be identified as the Author and
Heather Heyworth to be identified as the Illustrator of this Work have been
asserted by them in accordance with the Copyright, Designs and Patents Act, 1988.

Series Editor: Louise John
Editor: Katie Powell
Cover design: Paul Cherrill
Design: D.R.ink
Consultant: Shirley Bickler

A CIP catalogue record for this book is available from the British Library.

ISBN 9780750259279 (hbk)
ISBN 9780750260343 (pbk)

Printed in China

Wayland is a division of Hachette Children's Books,
an Hachette UK Company

www.hachette.co.uk

Skipping in the Street

Written by Anna Matthew
Illustrated by Heather Heyworth

WAYLAND

My sisters and I
liked skipping.

We played skipping
in the street.

The postman came along.

"That looks fun. Can
I jump in?" he said.

Then a boy came up
the street.

He liked skipping
so he jumped in.

A man walked up
the street.

"That looks fun. Can
I jump in?" he said.

Then the milkman
came along.

He liked skipping
so he jumped in.

A dustbin man came up
the street.

"Can I jump in?" he said.
"I like skipping!"

Then a policeman
came along.

He looked at us all.

"**No more skipping!**"
he said.

So the postman,
the boy,
the man,
the milkman,
and the dustbin man...

...all went skipping away!

Guiding a First Read of
Skipping in the Street

It is important to talk through the book with the child before they read it alone. This prepares them for the way the story unfolds, and allows them to enjoy the pictures as you both talk naturally, using the language they will later encounter when reading. Read them the brief overview below, and then follow the suggestions:

1. Talking through the book
The girl and her sisters like to play skipping in the street. She tells us about the time when lots of people came along and jumped in, too.

> Let's read the title: **Skipping in the Street**
> Let's look at the pictures.
> Here on page 4 is the girl and her sisters.
> She says, "We like skipping."
> Who came along on the next page?
> Yes, the postman. He said, "That looks fun."
> And on page 8 a boy came up the street.
> He jumped in, too.

Continue through the book, guiding the discussion to fit the text as the child looks at the illustrations.

> On page 16, a policeman came along.
> He thought there was too much skipping.
> So the people — here they are on the last
> page — all went skipping away!

2. A first reading of the book

Ask the child to read the book independently, pointing carefully under each word (tracking) while thinking about the story. Praise attempts by the child to correct themselves, and prompt them to use their letter knowledge, the punctuation and check the meaning, for example:

I liked the way you checked the picture and sounded out that word and then read the sentence again to check that it made sense.

Did you spot that question mark?
Try it again so that it sounds like a question.

3. Follow-up activities

The high frequency words in this title are:
came   can   he   I   in   like   look   man   said   the

- Select two high frequency words, and ask the child or group to find them throughout the book. Discuss the shape of the letters and the letter sounds.
- To memorise the words, ask the child to write them in the air, then write them repeatedly on a whiteboard or on paper, leaving a space between each attempt.

4. Encourage

- Reading the book again – with expression.
- Drawing a picture based on the story.
- Writing one or two sentences using the practised words.

23

START READING is a series of highly enjoyable books for beginner readers. **The books have been carefully graded to match the Book Bands widely used in schools.** This enables readers to be sure they choose books that match their own reading ability.

Look out for the Band colour on the book in our Start Reading logo.

The Bands are:

Pink Band 1A & 1B

Red Band 2

Yellow Band 3

Blue Band 4

Green Band 5

Orange Band 6

Turquoise Band 7

Purple Band 8

Gold Band 9

START READING books can be read independently or shared with an adult. They promote the enjoyment of reading through satisfying stories supported by fun illustrations.

Anna Matthew loves writing stories about when she was a child. She lived in a seaside town and spent lots of time playing on the beach, and in the park and street. Now her two children are growing up, and she can write about their fun and games, too!

Heather Heyworth lives in Suffolk with her husband, two children and a very demanding cat called Wooster!